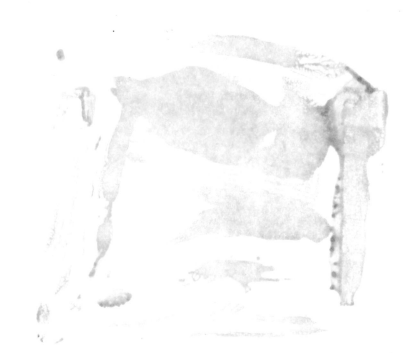

Word  Bird™

Asks:
What? What? What?

Published in the United States of America by The Child's World®, Inc.
PO Box 326
Chanhassen, MN 55317-0326
800-599-READ
www.childsworld.com

Project Manager Mary Berendes
Editor Katherine Stevenson, Ph.D.
Designer Ian Butterworth

Library of Congress Cataloging-in-Publication Data
Moncure, Jane Belk.
Word Bird asks: What? What? What? / by Jane Belk Moncure.
p. cm.
Summary: While taking a walk with this father, Word Bird
asks lots of questions about the things he sees.
ISBN 1-56766-994-8 (lib. : alk. paper)
[1. Questions and answers—Fiction. 2. Birds—Fiction.]   I. Title.
PZ7.M739 Wm 2002
[E]—dc21
2001006040

Word Bird™

Asks:
What? What? What?

by Jane Belk Moncure
illustrated by Chris McEwan

One day, Word Bird and
Papa went for a walk.

They walked to a pond.
"What is in the pond?"
asked Word Bird.

"Let's find out," said Papa.

They found

frogs,

tadpoles,

and ducks.

What else?

Then they walked
in the woods.

"What is in the woods?"
asked Word Bird.

"Let's find out," said Papa.

They found

acorns,

a raccoon,

and a little deer.

What else?

Word Bird and Papa walked into a field.

"What is in the field?"
 asked Word Bird.
"Let's find out," said Papa.

They found daisies...

lots of daisies.

They also found

 butterflies,

a bunny,

and grasshoppers.

What else?

They came to a farm.

"What is on the farm?"
asked Word Bird.

"Let's find out," said Papa.

They found a
cow and a calf,…

a hen,

a mother pig and piglets,

sheep,

and lambs.

What else?

Papa and Word Bird
walked down the road.

"What was that?"
asked Word Bird.

Mama was in the truck.

"Let's have a picnic,"
she said.

"What is in the picnic basket?" asked Word Bird.

"Let's find out," said Papa.

They found
sandwiches,

apples,

a pickle,

and carrot sticks.

What else?

After the picnic,
Word Bird asked,
"What will we do now?"

"Let's go to the zoo,"
said Mama.

"What is in the zoo?"
asked Word Bird.

"Let's find out," said Papa.

They found monkeys,...

a giraffe,

a yak,

a camel,

and polar bears.

What else?

"Let's get some ice cream," said Papa.

Word Bird did not ask,
"What? What? What?"

Word Bird knew
just what to get…

a chocolate
and cherry
and vanilla
and strawberry
ice cream cone!

Can you read these words with Word Bird?

tadpoles

pickle

chipmunk

calf

acorns

sandwiches

daisies

basket

grasshopper

camel

raccoon

polar bear